WATER WORLD

Contents

Haydn Middleton

Story illustrated by
Seb Burnett

Before Reading

Find out about

- One of the world's longest rivers – the Amazon, in South America

Tricky words

- season
- Australia
- medicines
- canoe
- Manaus
- piranha
- anaconda

Introduce these tricky words and help the reader when they come across them later!

Text starter

The Amazon is a very wide river. It flows from the Andes Mountains to the Atlantic Ocean. Along the Amazon you can find amazing rainforest trees, dangerous fish, like the piranha, and really dangerous snakes, like the anaconda.

Amazing Amazon

River without a Bridge

There are no bridges over the Amazon.

Why not? It's too wide!

If you stand on one side of the Amazon, you cannot see the other side. Amazing!

Who are you calling Big Mouth?

The Amazon is in South America.

It starts high up in the Andes.

Then it flows down, down, down,

until it gets to the Atlantic Ocean.

It flows down for *thousands* of miles.

Have you ever heard people say,
"You've got a big mouth"?
You could say that to the Amazon!

mouth of river

Every river has a mouth.
It is where it flows into the sea.
The mouth of the Amazon is
hundreds of miles wide.
What a big mouth!

Rain tops up the River

The Amazon has more water in it than any other river!

In the rainy season the Amazon has even more water in it because the rain tops up the river level.

When it rains near the Amazon it *really* rains. It pours and pours.

After really heavy rain, the river level rises and rises.
The water spills over the river banks and floods the land around it.
It can even flood over the tops of the trees!

There are hundreds of islands like this one near the mouth of the Amazon.

Amazon Rainforest

Lots of plants grow in rainy places and even more grow in *hot* rainy places. Near the Amazon it's *really* hot and *really* rainy. So that is where the world's biggest rainforest grows. It's as big as Australia!

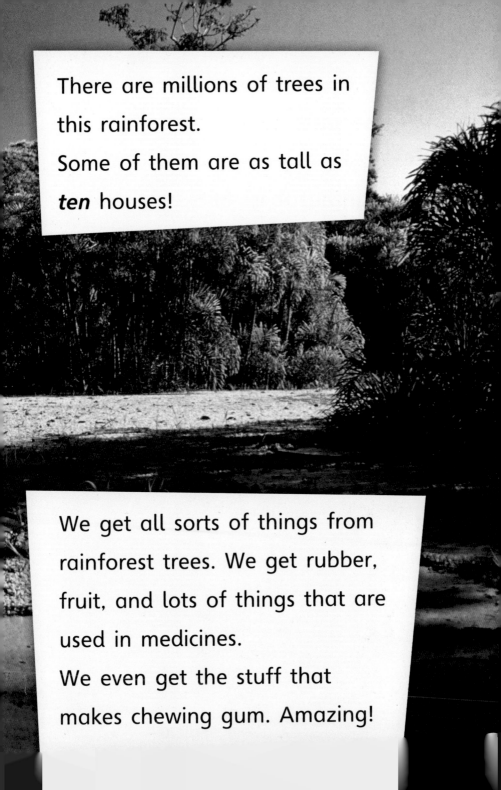

There are millions of trees in this rainforest.
Some of them are as tall as *ten* houses!

We get all sorts of things from rainforest trees. We get rubber, fruit, and lots of things that are used in medicines.
We even get the stuff that makes chewing gum. Amazing!

Living on the Amazon

Lots of people live and work on the Amazon. Most families do not have a car, but they do have a canoe. They use the canoe like we use a car. The Amazon is like a big wide road!

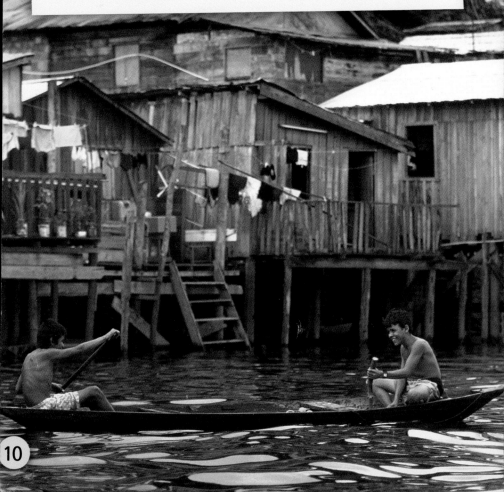

Some families live in a big city called Manaus.

Every day, at 3pm, rain pours down for an hour. Then the rain stops and the sun comes out and everything dries up really quickly. Amazing!

Just Look What's in the Water!

The most dangerous fish in the Amazon is the piranha.

When a big boat tipped over on the Amazon, three hundred people fell in the river ... and never got out.

Why not? The *piranhas* ate them!

The local name for the river dolphin is 'boto'.

But what eats piranhas?

River dolphins eat piranhas.

Most dolphins live in the sea but river dolphins live in the Amazon.

They swim up to the piranha and swallow them in one go. Amazing!

All sorts of snakes live in the rainforest. The anaconda is a really dangerous snake. It can eat an animal bigger than itself. It swallows it in one go!

After a meal like that, anacondas don't need to eat again for months! That is *really* amazing!

Text Detective

- What dangerous animals are found in the Amazon?
- Would you like to live in the rainforest?

Word Detective

- **Phonic Focus:** Doubling consonants
  Page 12: What must be added to 'tip' before you can add 'ed'?
- Page 3: Why does the word 'Amazon' have a capital letter?
- Page 8: Find a word meaning the opposite of 'cold'.

Super Speller

Read these words:

never   things   tipped

Now try to spell them!

HA! HA! HA!

Q Where does a river keep its money?

A In a river bank.

In this story

 Schoolboy Mo who is also Mole Man

 The Big Slug, his arch enemy

 Piranha fish

 Prince Anaconda

Tricky words

- twitching
- ordinary
- underground
- rainforest
- Amazon
- jacuzzi

Introduce these tricky words and help the reader when they come across them later!

Story starter

Mo is no ordinary boy. He has a very special nose. And when he smells trouble, something amazing happens – Mo turns into a super-hero called Mole Man! One day, the class was going swimming when Mo smelled bad trouble. Could it be his arch enemy, the Big Slug?

Mole Man
up the
Amazon

Mo's class was going swimming.

"The bus is leaving in one minute,"
said the teacher.

Just then, Mo's nose started twitching.

Mo had a special nose. He could smell trouble anywhere in the world. And he smelled *bad* trouble now. "Please can I get my bag from the classroom?" asked Mo, and he ran off.

Mo rushed to his secret spot – and he burst out of his school clothes.

Mo was not an ordinary boy any more.

Mo was now ... **Mole Man!**

"Sniff, sniff," went Mole Man.

"Time to go digging!"

So Mole Man set off underground
to find the trouble.

He dug faster than the speed of light!

Mole Man dug under land and sea.
"I bet the Big Slug is behind this
trouble," he said. "But Mole Man can
sort it out."
Soon his nose was twitching really fast.
"Sniff, sniff," went Mole Man.
"Time to tunnel *up*."

A moment later he burst up through the ground.

He was in a rainforest, next to the mighty Amazon River.

But there was hardly any water in the river!

"Mole Man!" said some piranha fish. "You've come at just the right time. We're in terrible trouble. The Big Slug is building the world's biggest jacuzzi. And he's taking our river water to fill it up!"

Would you like to go in a jacuzzi?

"Sniff," went Mole Man.

"I thought I smelled the Big Slug and I can hear him having fun in his jacuzzi."

"What can we do, Mole Man?"
asked the piranha fish.
Just then, Mole Man saw a huge pipe.
"That pipe is sucking your river water
into the jacuzzi," he said. "We have
to get rid of it."

"But we're not strong enough!"
said the piranha fish. "We need help!"

"I can help you," said Prince Anaconda.

"Excellent!" said Mole Man. "Climb on to that branch over the river."
Prince Anaconda did just that.
"Now what?" he asked.

"Wrap yourself around the pipe," said Mole Man. Prince Anaconda did just that. "Now pull the pipe up," said Mole Man. Prince Anaconda pulled. Up, up, up ... Suddenly there was a huge **CRACK**!

Prince Anaconda had snapped
the pipe!

Soon the river was filling up again.

"Nice work, Mole Man!" said the
piranha fish.

But someone else *wasn't* happy.

The Big Slug was very cross.

"My jacuzzi is empty!" he cried.

"This must be the work of Mole Man!

I'm coming to get you, Mole Man!"

But first he had to get across the river.

And that was a problem – because the

Big Slug couldn't swim!

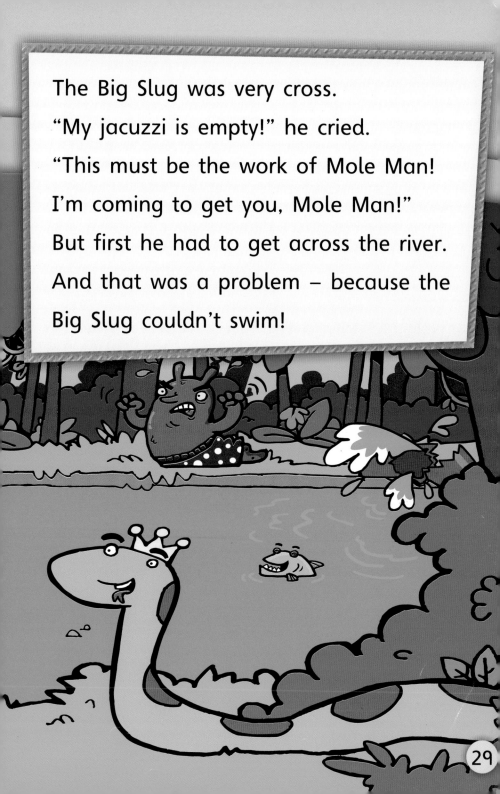

"Can't you find your armbands?"
shouted Mole Man.
Then he turned to Prince Anaconda
and the piranha fish.
"Thank you," they said.
"No problem," said Mole Man.
Then he dug all the way back to school
and changed into his school clothes.

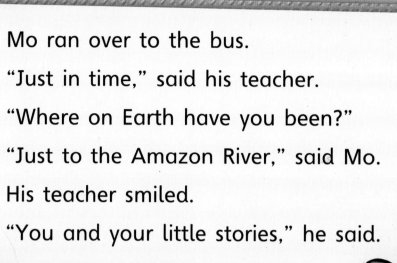

Mo ran over to the bus.

"Just in time," said his teacher.

"Where on Earth have you been?"

"Just to the Amazon River," said Mo.

His teacher smiled.

"You and your little stories," he said.

Quiz

Text Detective

- Why had the Big Slug taken the water from the Amazon?
- Do you think the teacher believed Mo's excuse?

Word Detective

- **Phonic Focus:** Doubling consonants
  Page 17: What must be added to 'swim' before you can add 'ing'?
- Page 17: What did the teacher say to the class?
- Page 28: Why is the word 'wasn't' in italics?

Super Speller

Read these words:

swimming   wasn't   snapped

Now try to spell them!

HA! HA! HA!

Q What grows bigger the more you take from it?

A A hole.